CONTE

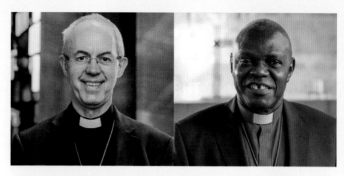

INTRODUCTION

Jesus Christ gave the most beautiful and powerful talk the world has ever heard: the Sermon on the Mount. These words have shaped history and turned many people's lives inside out.

Right at the beginning are eight short sayings which all begin with the word 'Blessed'.

These sayings are a portrait of Jesus, the Son of God. They answer the deepest question of our age: what does it mean to be human?

For some they will be a very simple introduction to Jesus. For others they will be a way of going deeper. Some will read them in Lent, but they can be used at any time of year. Some will use them to prepare for baptism and confirmation. Others to go deeper in the Way of Christ.

However you take this *Pilgrim Journey*, make space. Allow God's word to dwell in you richly as we seek together as a Church to know Jesus better and to become more Christ-like in everything we are and in everything we do.

Archbishops Justin Welby and John Sentamu

HOW TO USE THIS BOOK

Pilgrim Journeys: The Beatitudes is ideal for anyone to use daily in Lent – starting from Ash Wednesday* and finishing 40 days later on Palm Sunday – but it can be used at any time of year.

The 40 daily reflections on The Beatitudes are grouped in eight chapters of five days on each beatitude. Each day offers:

- A **theme** linked to the beatitude
- A suggested short Bible **reading** that explores that theme
- An invitation to **reflect**
- A suggestion of how to **pray**
- A prompt to **act**.

Across each group of five days we will explore what each beatitude tells us about Jesus, what it tells us about a vision for human life and the life of the Church.

At the end, you will find some possible next steps for you on your discipleship journey as well as some further resources including other *Pilgrim* materials for you to explore.

Those preparing for baptism or confirmation may find this *Pilgrim Journey* helpful as part of their preparation for that commitment. Members of *Pilgrim* groups spending six weeks exploring *The Beatitudes* (Book 4) together could use this daily material in between sessions.

* Ash Wednesday falls on the following dates over the coming years: 6 March in 2019; 26 February in 2020; 17 February in 2021; 2 March in 2022; 22 February in 2023; 14 February in 2024.

A SHORT GUIDE TO THE BEATITUDES

The Pilgrim Way: A short guide to the Christian Faith explores what it means to share and live out our faith and identity as followers of Jesus Christ. It is shaped around four core Christian texts, including The Beatitudes.

This extract from *The Pilgrim Way* summarizes why these words of Jesus have been so important to the life of Christians down the ages. You might like to read this before you embark on the daily reflections, and perhaps re-visit it each week, or even try learning it by heart.

. . . .

Pilgrim, what is the Christian vision for the world?

The Christian vision for the world is one where God reigns in justice, peace and love.

. . . .

How does Jesus Christ describe the citizens of God's kingdom?

Jesus Christ said this to the crowds who followed him. They are known as the Beatitudes:

THE BEATITUDES

Blessed are the poor in spirit,
for theirs is the kingdom of heaven.

Blessed are those who mourn,
for they shall be comforted.

Blessed are the meek,
for they shall inherit the earth.

Blessed are those who hunger
and thirst after righteousness,
for they shall be satisfied.

Blessed are the merciful,
for they shall obtain mercy.

Blessed are the pure in heart,
for they shall see God.

Blessed are the peacemakers,
for they shall be called children of God.

Blessed are those who suffer
persecution for righteousness' sake,
for theirs is the kingdom of heaven.

Matthew 5.3–10

What do we learn from these Beatitudes about the life of the kingdom? We learn that we are blessed when we know our need of God, when we weep with compassion for the needs of the world, when we share God's longing for justice and peace, and when we clothe ourselves with mercy and grace.

What is the cost of the life of the kingdom? Jesus Christ says that if any want to be his disciples, let them deny themselves, take up their cross daily and follow him.

What does it mean to carry the cross? In baptism, Christians receive the sign of the cross. We encourage one another to fight valiantly against sin, the world and the devil, and to remain faithful to Christ to the end of our life.

What is the hope in which a Christian lives? A Christian lives in the sure and certain hope that as Jesus Christ rose from the dead, so he will come again in glory to judge the world. Christians believe that God will renew the heavens and the earth, and that beyond death we will enjoy eternal life with God.

DAYS 1 TO 5

'BLESSED ARE THE POOR IN SPIRIT, FOR THEIRS IS THE KINGDOM OF HEAVEN'

DAY 1
EIGHT BLESSINGS

READ Matthew 5.1–10

*'Blessed are the poor in spirit,
for theirs is the kingdom of heaven.'*

. . . .

REFLECT

Welcome to this 40-day journey. Like the first
disciples, we are making time to listen to the words
of Jesus.

At the beginning of the most famous sermon in
history – known as the Sermon on the Mount –
Jesus commends eight beautiful qualities.
These are almost his first words and the very
heart of his teaching.

Each *quality* is set within a *blessing*. Every blessing is set within a *promise*. These are words of joy and hope.

We will take five days to think about each blessing. The eight blessings will help us come to know Jesus better. They are a kind of miniature portrait, unpacked in the four gospels.

The same eight blessings will give us a vision for what it means to be fully alive, to live as God intends, both as individuals and as a community.

. . . .

PRAY

Still your mind. Take time to listen to the words of Jesus and repeat them several times with the rhythm of your breathing:

*'Blessed are the poor in spirit,
for theirs is the kingdom of heaven.'*

. . . .

ACT

How will you set aside time and space for reflection and listening through these 40 days?

A RHYTHM OF LIFE

READ Luke 5.12–16

'But he would withdraw to deserted places and pray...'

. . . .

REFLECT

One of the greatest needs in our 24/7 world is to learn to withdraw and reconnect with God.

Jesus himself knows his need of God. His life is lived in a rhythm of full engagement with God's world alternating by withdrawing to deserted places to pray.

Jesus prays in the great crises of his life – before great miracles and before his arrest and trial. But these prayers grow out of his daily prayer and conversation with his Father in heaven. He models what it means to be poor in spirit.

Luke tells us, 'But he would withdraw to deserted places and pray.' To follow Jesus is to recognize this inner thirst for the living God. To follow Jesus and to be poor in spirit is to find this life-giving rhythm.

. . . .

PRAY

As the deer longs for the water brooks,
so longs my soul for you, O God.
My soul is athirst for God,
even for the living God.
Psalm 42

. . . .

ACT

What is your best time of day to pray? How can you create the time and space?

DAY 3
BELOVED

READ Matthew 3.13–17

'And a voice from heaven said, "This is my Son, the Beloved, with whom I am well pleased."'

. . . .

REFLECT

Many of us today no longer know who we really are or what our lives are truly worth. These deep questions can eat away at our peace of mind.

Baptism is at the centre of the Christian understanding of who we are and what our lives mean. Jesus begins his public ministry at his baptism by John in the Jordan. As Jesus comes out of the water, he receives the gift of the Spirit and hears these powerful words of life: 'This is my Son, the Beloved, with whom I am well pleased.'

Jesus' life and identity flow from understanding that he is the Son of God and dearly loved by God. He knows his need of God right at the beginning and continues to walk in this way.

PRAY

Listen to God's words to you in Christ:

'My child, my Beloved,
with whom I am well pleased.'

. . . .

ACT

Is this a season in your life to seek baptism, or to confirm or renew the promises made at your baptism?

EMPTY HANDS

READ Luke 18.9–14

'God, be merciful to me, a sinner!'

. . . .

REFLECT

Many people think that to live well is to be self-sufficient. But life is impoverished without vulnerability – without the love of God and of others. Coming to God full of ourselves is the opposite of what it means to be poor in spirit. The Pharisee in Jesus' story is like this: superior in everything.

The tax-collector comes with empty hands. He stands far off, eyes cast down, beats his breast and prays, 'God, be merciful to me, a sinner!' This is what it means to be poor in spirit. It is the tax-collector who finds the kingdom of heaven. Jesus says, 'This man went down to his home justified rather than the other.'

If we come to God full of ourselves, we cannot receive anything. Our prayers are boastful. It's all about our reputationbefore others.

So we come with empty hands.

. . . .

PRAY

Pray, today, with empty hands:

'God, be merciful to me, a sinner!'

. . . .

ACT

Try saying the tax-collector's prayer or the Lord's Prayer twice: once with your hands full and once with your hands open and empty.

DAY 5
THE BETTER PART

READ Luke 10.38–42

*'you are worried and distracted by
many things; there is need of only
one thing.'*

. . . .

REFLECT

Anxiety and fear accumulate in people,
in families and communities. We can be
anxious about our appearance, about what
others think, about whether life is fair,
about our past or our future. Anxiety can
steal joy, calm and fulfilment.

Martha is entertaining one of her closest
friends. Yet she is worried and distracted by
many things – an image of many people's
lives and, too often, of the Church.

Mary is poor in spirit. She sits at Jesus' feet
and listens to what he is saying. She has

chosen the better part. It will not be taken from her.

We cannot escape our past, our worries or our sense of emptiness on our own. Help is at hand as we admit our need of God in poverty of Spirit and find the kingdom of heaven.

. . . .

PRAY

Imagine yourself sitting at the feet of Jesus and spend some time listening to what he is saying.

. . . .

ACT

How will you live out Mary's priorities and attitude in your daily life?

DAYS 6 TO 10

'BLESSED ARE THOSE WHO MOURN, FOR THEY SHALL BE COMFORTED'

COMPASSION

READ Matthew 5.1–10

'Blessed are those who mourn,
for they shall be comforted.'

. . . .

REFLECT

We will return every five days to these
eight beautiful attitudes: this portrait of
Jesus and of life in all its fullness.

'Blessed are those who mourn' is a word
for every Christian, not just a comfort to the
bereaved. There is a huge paradox here
which is meant to make us think. Happiness
('Blessed') is next to sorrow. Grief is set in
the context of hope.

We live in a world full of suffering and loss.
To mourn is to be courageous. We dare to
open our eyes and ears and hearts to the

suffering around us and the pain within us.

To grieve in this way is only possible because of God's love and God's hope – otherwise the pain and suffering would overwhelm us. Jesus offers us the only way to live well: to open our eyes to suffering yet hold that pain within God's greater love and joy.

. . . .

PRAY

Still your mind. Take time to listen to the words of Jesus and repeat them several times with the rhythm of your breathing:

'Blessed are those who mourn,
for they shall be comforted.'

. . . .

ACT

Make a list of the five things which most grieve you in the world today. Share it with someone and ask for their list in return.

DAY 7
COMPASSION IN ACTION
READ Mark 1.40–45

'Moved with pity...'

. . . .

REFLECT

Jesus knows his need of God: his life reflects his poverty of spirit. Jesus' life also reflects his grief at the pain and distress in the world.

In this passage and many others, Jesus is deeply moved by the suffering of others. Something stirs deep within. We will go on to read of his love for poor and rich, for Gentiles and Jews, for old and young, for men and women, for sinners and for the righteous.

That love is often shown in his tears, in mourning and frustration which springs from compassion. The compassion is expressed first in the gift of attention: turning aside from this day's tasks to understand another's distress. The compassion becomes then prayer and practical help – bringing hope and good news.

God enters into the pain of our world through the tears of his Son. Through those tears we understand God's love for all who experience pain and loss in every age and land.

PRAY

Pray for the situations and people you met or heard of yesterday that move you within.

ACT

What act of mercy or attention can you offer today in response to that grief?

DAY 8
SORROW AND JOY

READ John 11.28–35

'Jesus began to weep...'

. . . .

REFLECT

Jesus breaks down our false pictures of God. God is not remote or far off or cold. God is near and with us in our suffering and reaches out to us in love.

Jesus stands at the tomb of Lazarus his friend. He sees the grief of Martha and Mary and the pain of the crowd. He is greatly disturbed in spirit and deeply moved. He, too, begins to weep. Immense power combines with deep vulnerability.

Death spoils and corrupts our lives and robs us of those we love. Grief is the most bitter pain we know. But death, our enemy, does not have the last word.

Jesus comes to give his life so that the power of death is broken. The raising of Lazarus is a sign of a greater resurrection: Jesus will rise on the third day and open the way for all people to inherit eternal life.

Blessed are those who mourn, for they shall be comforted.

. . . .

PRAY

*On the third day he rose again;
he ascended into heaven, he is seated at
the right hand of the Father, and he will
come to judge the living and the dead.*
The Apostles' Creed

. . . .

ACT

On the stroke of each hour today, remember the hope of resurrection. Notice what difference this makes.

DAY 9
FOLLOWING JESUS

READ Luke 10.25–37

'when he saw him he was moved with pity...'

. . . .

REFLECT

The world gives us an image of the good life: to live apart from poverty, to be blind to pain and suffering and pretend they do not exist.

Jesus offers a different way: to face the truth of loss and pain, to be moved with pity and to allow that love to shape our lives and actions.

The story of the Good Samaritan has rebuked and challenged the world since it was first crafted in response to the profound question: 'Who is my neighbour?'

The priest and the Levite have lost the capacity to mourn. They are blind to the pain of others. Only the Samaritan is moved with pity. His compassion moves him to action: he provides first aid, offers practical and financial support, and enlists the help of others.

This is the life to which Christ calls his followers: the life shaped by mercy and compassion and mourning.

. . . .

PRAY

Pray for those who will cross your path today by chance who need mercy and grace.

. . . .

ACT

Take down some of the inner walls which insulate you from the suffering of others.

DAY 10
THE LAST WORD OF ALL

READ Romans 8.35–39

'Who will separate us from the love of Christ?'

. . . .

REFLECT

One of the greatest challenges of living well is to hold together joy and pain: to acknowledge life's challenges and difficulties but not to be overwhelmed or twisted by them.

The second beatitude shows us the way. We are to open eyes, ears and hearts to our own suffering and the suffering of others. But we hold that pain and difficulty in the deeper, wider, higher frame of God's immeasurable love shown in Jesus Christ, his Son. In that love, every hurt will be healed, every tear turn to joy, every night give way to a new dawn.

Paul tells us that nothing in all creation can or will separate us from the love of Christ. Here is a truth to take hold of daily that runs through the worship of the Christian family – the Church.

The Church is called each day to joy, but the kind of joy which holds and embraces suffering and pain in the world and in the Church.

. . . .

PRAY

O come, let us sing to the Lord;
let us heartily rejoice
in the rock of our salvation.
Let us come into his presence
with thanksgiving
and be glad in him with psalms.
Psalm 95

. . . .

ACT

Learn Romans 8.38 by heart and say it each night before you go to sleep this week.

DAYS 11 TO 15

'BLESSED ARE
THE MEEK,
FOR THEY SHALL
INHERIT THE
EARTH'

DAY 11
MEEKNESS

READ Matthew 5.1–10

'Blessed are the meek, for they shall inherit the earth.'

. . . .

REFLECT

Jesus is poor in spirit, knowing his need of God. He mourns with compassion for the pain of the world.

This third face of the portrait takes us to a third quality at the heart of the character of Jesus: humility. Jesus stands in the long line of servants of God which stretches back to Moses, who was 'more humble than anyone on the face of the earth' (Numbers 14.2).

As we will see, Jesus models meekness and the way of a servant throughout the gospels. Jesus commends the life of service to his disciples. The early Church was quick to see humility at the very heart of God's Son becoming a person: 'he emptied himself, taking the form of a slave, being born in human likeness' (Philippians 2.7).

Meekness is not to be confused with weakness, however. There is real strength in Jesus, combined with humility before God and others.

. . . .

PRAY

Still your mind. Take time to listen to the words of Jesus and repeat them several times with the rhythm of your breathing:

'Blessed are the meek,
for they shall inherit the earth.'

. . . .

ACT

What examples would you give from history or public life – or people you know – of true humility?

WASHING FEET

READ John 13.1–15

'he poured water into a basin and began to wash the disciples' feet...'

· ·

REFLECT

It is an extraordinary moment. John tells us that Jesus knows 'that the Father has given all things into his hands'. This is God the Son dwelling among us. How does God the Son show us what God is like?

He ties a towel around himself, pours water into a basin and begins to wash the disciples' feet. Extraordinary service in a remarkable moment – Jesus' last meal with his disciples before he is crucified.

This is what God's love means. Jesus serves and ministers to his disciples in the offer of cleansing and forgiveness, in daily friendship and care, in modelling the good and life-giving way.

John invites us to hold together in our minds the God who created the heavens and the earth and

the gentle teacher kneeling at the feet of his friends at the end of a long and tiring day. They are one and the same.

. . . .

PRAY

Wash me thoroughly from my wickedness and cleanse me from my sin.
Psalm 51

. . . .

ACT

Attempt to live one day as a servant, washing the feet of those you come into contact with. What do you learn?

DAY 13
GREATNESS

READ Matthew 20.20–27
'It will not be so among you...'

. . . .

REFLECT

The urge to be first and be number one is very strong. It drives careers, poisons families, ruins friendships and works against true human flourishing. We tread one another down to get to the top.

The story of James and John shows the same attitude among the disciples (and their families).

Jesus rebukes them in words which are unforgettable: 'It will not be so among you.'

Greatness in God's household is a race to the bottom, not a race to the top. Humility, not status, is the key to joy and satisfaction. The one who chases power or position can never be content. Even when we reach the top (however we define it), anxiety about staying there steals our peace.

The way of humility and meekness is counter-cultural. But the way of the servant is also the way of joy and surrender and true fulfilment.

. . . .

PRAY

O Lord my heart is not proud;
my eyes are not raised in haughty looks...
But I have quieted and stilled my soul,
like a weaned child on its mother's breast;
so is my soul quieted within me.
Psalm 131

. . . .

ACT

Carry out at least one secret act of service today to bless someone in your work or home life.

DAY 14
THANKSGIVING

READ Luke 17.11–19

'Was none found to return and give thanks except this foreigner?'

. . . .

REFLECT

Ten leprosy sufferers come to seek healing. All are made clean but only one – a Samaritan – returns to Jesus to give thanks.

A thankful heart is the flipside of the coin of meekness. The two go together. Those who live in selfishness and pride so easily miss God's blessings: the everyday joys of creation, of family and friends, of simple pleasures. Our narrow hearts look always for what's not right or for that one thing more. Contentment vanishes like morning mist.

A meek heart is a wider and wilder heart, broadened and deepened by thanksgiving and praise. Praise and thanksgiving are daily disciplines for Christians – key spiritual exercises in meekness.

In praise we bow before God and remember our place in the world. In thanksgiving we rehearse and enjoy all that God has given us. The meek not so much inherit the earth as remember to enjoy it.

. . . .

PRAY

We bless thee for our creation, preservation, and all the blessings of this life; but above all for thine inestimable love in the redemption of the world by our Lord Jesus Christ, for the means of grace, and for the hope of glory.
from A General Thanksgiving, The Book of Common Prayer

. . . .

ACT

Try and learn by heart the General Thanksgiving and use it each day.

DAY 15
NEW CLOTHES

READ Colossians 3.9–15

'clothe yourselves with compassion, kindness, humility, meekness, and patience...'

. . . .

REFLECT

Baptism is full of rich pictures of the Christian life. This part of Colossians focusses on the idea of new clothes. The new Christians come to the waters of baptism and strip off their old garments – symbols of the life they leave behind.

They go down into the waters of baptism and rise up to a new life. As they come out of the water each is given new clothes. Colossians says these clothes are like Christian qualities which need to be put on each day. They are the qualities of Christ himself. Among them are humility, meekness and patience, the focus of our beatitude.

As Christian disciples we never grow out of our baptism. Each day, together as a community, we return to the profound actions of dying to our old self and rising to new life; of putting off our old attitudes and putting on Christ again.

· ·

PRAY

I bind unto myself today
the strong name of the Trinity,
by invocation of the same,
the Three in One, and One in Three.
from St Patrick's Breastplate

· ·

ACT

Think of the most challenging situation for you to exercise humility, whether at home, work, church or some other context. Each time you enter or leave that place, deliberately put on meekness like a garment.

DAYS 16 TO 20

'BLESSED ARE THOSE WHO HUNGER AND THIRST AFTER RIGHTEOUSNESS, FOR THEY SHALL BE SATISFIED'

JESUS THE PROPHET

READ Matthew 5.1–10

'Blessed are those who hunger and thirst after righteousness, for they shall be satisfied.'

. . . .

REFLECT

The portrait of Jesus is given a fourth dimension. Jesus is hungry and thirsty for righteousness.

In the third beatitude about meekness, Jesus puts himself in the long line of Israel's kings. The ideal king would enter the city humble and riding on a donkey (Matthew 21.5, quoting Zechariah 9.9).

In the fourth, Jesus places himself in the long line of the prophets – Elijah, Elisha, Amos and Isaiah – who long to see God's justice prevail.

The prophets hold to a powerful vision of what the world can and should be: a world in which the weak are protected, not exploited. Jesus describes this vision of a new world as the kingdom of God (or the kingdom of heaven in Matthew). The prophets often act out their message in powerful signs.

The gospels will show us that Jesus is a prophet in this long tradition – and even more than a prophet.

. . . .

PRAY

Still your mind. Take time to listen to the words of Jesus and repeat them several times with the rhythm of your breathing:

*'Blessed are those who hunger
and thirst after righteousness,
for they shall be satisfied.'*

. . . .

ACT

If you can, plan to fast one day this week in some way. Can you connect your hunger and thirst with a longing for justice?

DAY 17
GOOD NEWS

READ Luke 4.16–22

'he has anointed me to bring good news to the poor...'

. . . .

REFLECT

In Luke's gospel, the first public act of Jesus' ministry is here in the synagogue in Nazareth. Jesus reads a portion of the Book of Isaiah (mainly from Isaiah 61) as a kind of manifesto for his ministry.

Jesus' life is good news in action. The poor hear the good news. Captives are set free. The blind receive sight. The oppressed are delivered.

Each of these (and more) flows out of Jesus' hunger and thirst for justice – for the world to be as God intends it to be. The Christian faith is about far more than personal righteousness or seeking a place in heaven. Part of being a Christian is sharing this longing for the world to be set right, for God's kingdom to come. Part of being a Christian is believing that the kingdom will come one day and this deep longing will be satisfied.

. . . .

PRAY

I lift up my eyes to the hills;
from where is my help to come?
My help comes from the Lord,
the maker of heaven and earth.
Psalm 121

. . . .

ACT

Write your own short manifesto. How do you long for the world to be different?

CLEANSING THE TEMPLE

READ Mark 11.15–19

'My house shall be called a house of prayer for all the nations...'

. . . .

REFLECT

Prophets use signs and big public gestures to communicate. Sometimes those signs are miracles like the stilling of the storm or the feeding of the five thousand. Sometimes they are symbolic actions – a form of protest at the way things are and a longing for them to be different.

The story of Jesus cleansing the temple is a kind of symbolic action. For all the prophets, right action and right worship go together. Jesus is restoring the temple to what it should be: a place for everyone and especially a place for the poor.

If we are hungry and thirsty for justice then this will need to affect the way we live and the way we give. But our faith is more than a private matter. Seeking justice should also mean that we become actively involved in building a better world through campaigns and advocacy.

· ·

PRAY

Guide the leaders of the nations into the ways of peace and justice.
from the Litany

· ·

ACT

The fourth of 'The Five Marks of Mission' is:

'To seek to transform unjust structures of society, to challenge violence of every kind and pursue peace and reconciliation.'

How will you seek to live this out today?

SEVEN ACTS OF MERCY

READ Matthew 25.31–45

'as you did it to one of the least of these who are members of my family, you did it to me...'

. . . .

REFLECT

One day, God's kingdom of justice and peace will come. The world will be set right. Those who are hungry and thirsty for righteousness will be satisfied. All people will have to give account for the way we have lived.

The Church has taken the list of acts of kindness in this parable and fashioned them into Seven Acts of Mercy (a list similar to the Seven Virtues or the Seven Deadly Sins). They are to:

1. Feed the hungry
2. Give water to the thirsty
3. Clothe the naked
4. Shelter the homeless
5. Visit the sick

6. Visit the imprisoned
7. Bury the dead
   (added to the list in the parable).

The richest life is not to live for ourselves but to live for others. The Church is called to be a community that lives out these acts of mercy and kindness as part of the life of every disciple.

. . . .

PRAY

Lord, make me an instrument of your peace.
Where there is hatred, let me sow love;
where there is injury, pardon;
where there is doubt, faith;
where there is despair, hope...
A Franciscan Prayer

. . . .

ACT

Are you able to do something today which is one of the Seven Acts of Mercy?

DAY 20
A COMMUNITY OF GRACE

READ Romans 12.9–21

'Do not be overcome by evil, but overcome evil with good.'

....

REFLECT

Most people are born with an innate sense of fairness. We begin our lives wanting the world to be a better place. Jesus affirms this in the fourth beatitude.

In too many cases, selfishness, apathy and cynicism dull this natural sense of justice. But Jesus stirs us to nurture this hunger and thirst for what is right and to set it as the compass for our daily lives.

But how? The world around us mostly lives a different way.

We must learn to swim against the tide. Paul recognizes that the best and only way to do that is in community. We need each other. We learn and practise virtue in the life of the Church.

Together we seek to grow more like Christ so that we can live as Christ's body in the world, as salt and light.

Together we are called not to be overcome by evil, but to overcome evil with good.

. . . .

PRAY

Teach us, good Lord, to serve as you deserve;
to give and not to count the cost;
to fight and not to heed the wounds;
to toil and not to seek for rest;
to labour and not to seek for any reward,
save that of knowing that we do your will.
Ignatius of Loyola (1556)

. . . .

ACT

Review the way you engage with your local church community. Are you involved enough to live out Romans 12 together?

DAYS 21 TO 25

'BLESSED ARE THE MERCIFUL, FOR THEY SHALL OBTAIN MERCY'

DAY 21
FORGIVENESS

READ Matthew 5.1–10

'Blessed are the merciful, for they shall obtain mercy.'

....

REFLECT

Jesus puts a remarkable emphasis in his ministry on forgiveness through both his teaching and his actions. Mercy in the Bible means strong and steadfast love from a stronger party in a relationship to a weaker one. It is shown first and foremost in forgiveness, which brings life and restores relationships, and then in acts of kindness and support.

This beautiful attitude will be echoed in the Lord's Prayer: 'Forgive us our sins as we forgive those who sin against us.' In Luke's gospel, this saying on mercy is followed almost immediately by a teaching on forgiveness: 'Forgive, and you will be forgiven; give, and it will be given to you' (Luke 6.36–37).

When Jesus demonstrates and lives out the mercy of God, he is speaking first about God's willingness to forgive when we fall short and go astray.

'Blessed are those who are willing to forgive, for they shall obtain forgiveness.'

. . . .

PRAY

Still your mind. Take time to listen to the words of Jesus and repeat them several times with the rhythm of your breathing:

'Blessed are the merciful,
for they shall obtain mercy.'

. . . .

ACT

Begin a list with two columns: people whom you need to forgive and people from whom you need to seek forgiveness. Be prepared to add to it during the next four days as you reflect on mercy.

DAY 22
EXTREME FORGIVENESS

READ Luke 23.32–43

'Father, forgive them; for they do not know what they are doing.'

. . . .

REFLECT

Jesus' words from the cross look back across the whole of the story of his passion. Jesus has been betrayed, arrested, tried, mocked, beaten and crucified.

As Jesus is lifted up and in agony, he is still able to forgive and to let go: 'Father, forgive them; for they do not know what they are doing.' Such is the mercy of God. Jesus is still able to reach out to one of those being crucified beside him: 'today you will be with me in paradise.'

At the last supper, Jesus gave a unique meaning to his death on the cross. He takes the cup and gives thanks. He gives it to the disciples saying: 'Drink from it, all of you; for this is my blood of the

covenant, which is poured out for many for the forgiveness of sins.'

Forgiveness and mercy are more than strong themes in the life and teaching of Jesus. They are the reason he offered his life.

. . . .

PRAY

Turn the words of the thief into your prayer today:

'Jesus, remember me when you come into your kingdom.' **Luke 23-42**

. . . .

ACT

Add a third column to your list: specific areas where you feel you need God's forgiveness and mercy.

DAY 23
MERCY IN ACTION

READ John 7.53–8.11

'Neither do I condemn you. Go your way, and from now on do not sin again.'

. . . .

REFLECT

The scribes and Pharisees bring to Jesus a woman found guilty of adultery. They use her to set a trap for him. He is tender and respectful and full of mercy.

Jesus is first silent and averts his gaze. He then turns the judgement back on the crowd: 'Let anyone among you who is without sin be the first to throw a stone at her.' We all have sinned in many different ways. We are all equally in need of the grace and mercy of God. We have no right to condemn others.

One by one they drift away, beginning with the elders. Jesus and the woman are left alone. Jesus extends forgiveness freely because of God's great love: 'Neither do I condemn you.'

This is the Saviour and Master we follow. This is the love God has for each person in creation. This is what it means to be merciful.

. . . .

PRAY

What shall I give you, Lord,
in return for all your kindness?
Glory to you for your love.
Glory to you for your patience.
Glory to you for forgiving all our sins.
Ephrem the Syrian (373)

. . . .

ACT

Review your list. Ask God to show you again the length, breadth, height and depth of his mercy and forgiveness for you.

SEVENTY TIMES SEVEN

READ Matthew 18.21–34

'if you do not forgive your brother or sister from your heart.'

. . . .

REFLECT

The world arounds us can suggest that the way to be happy is to think that we are perfect and everyone else is wrong. We should store up the wrongs that people do to us to bolster our own sense of being better.

Jesus tells us that the way to be happy is to be merciful: to remember that we are imperfect, that we need forgiveness every day, and that we need to extend that forgiveness to others and set them free.

Nelson Mandela once said: 'Resentment is like drinking poison and hoping it will kill your enemies.'

This powerful parable is told to the Church. Refusing to forgive poisons families, communities and workplaces. Small slights can grow into huge barriers.

One of the greatest gifts the Church has to offer the world around us is to be a community which practises this radical forgiveness, not seven times, but seventy times seven.

. . . .

PRAY

Christ be with me, Christ within me,
Christ behind me, Christ before me,
Christ beside me, Christ to win me,
Christ to comfort and restore me.
from St Patrick's Breastplate

. . . .

ACT

Look again at the three columns in your list. Do you need to extend them? Who are the people whom need to be forgiven 'seventy times seven'?

THE MERCY OF ANANIAS

READ Acts 9.10–18

'Brother Saul, the Lord Jesus…has sent me so that you may regain your sight…'

. . . .

REFLECT

The early Church practised extreme mercy and forgiveness. When Stephen becomes the first martyr, he echoes the words of Jesus on the cross: 'Lord do not hold this sin against them' (7.60). Saul approves of Stephen's death and devotes his life to the persecution of the Church.

The story of Saul's conversion on the road to

Damascus is well-known. Half the story is given to the way in which Ananias welcomes Saul, his persecutor, into the life of the Church.

Ananias' first word to Saul is a word of courage: 'Brother Saul'. Ananias prays for his enemy who has become his friend, prepares him for baptism and welcomes him into the life of the Church.

It is this quality of extreme mercy which gives the Church the ability to cross continents and to draw many to the fire of God's love. It is needed in every local church as we seek to welcome the sinner and the stranger.

. . . .

PRAY

O holy Jesus... most merciful redeemer, friend and brother, may we know you more clearly, love you more dearly, and follow you more nearly, day by day.
after Richard of Chichester (1253)

. . . .

ACT

Who are the people in your networks who need you to be like Ananias in the coming months?

DAYS 26 TO 30

'BLESSED ARE THE PURE IN HEART, FOR THEY SHALL SEE GOD'

DAY 26
INTEGRITY

READ Matthew 5.1–10
*'Blessed are the pure in heart,
for they shall see God.'*

....

REFLECT

Do we live from the outside in – to please others
and build our reputation in the eyes of the world?
Or do we live from the inside out – seeking to live
good, honest lives before God and leaving our
reputation in God's hands?

The sixth beatitude is about integrity. It is strong
medicine for a world bombarded by 24/7 social
media and struggling to keep its hold on truth.

It is also the best kind of good news for those who are weary of acting and keeping up appearances – the literal meaning of hypocrisy.

Jesus offers his own life as an example. He is observed at close quarters by friends and enemies. The four gospels, written within a generation or so of his resurrection, enable us to observe him, too. The more deeply we read them, the clearer his character becomes. What we see is what we get: God's love in human flesh.

. . . .

PRAY

Still your mind. Take time to listen to the words of Jesus and repeat them several times with the rhythm of your breathing:

'Blessed are the pure in heart,
for they shall see God.'

. . . .

ACT

Observe today how often you pretend to others in order to guard or build your reputation.

THE SECRET PLACE

READ Matthew 6.1–6, 16–18

'Beware of practising your piety before others in order to be seen by them; for then you have no reward from your Father in heaven.'

. . . .

REFLECT

To follow Jesus is to nurture your inner life in secret places and by hidden disciplines which no one knows but God.

There's a great temptation to parade our piety before others whether in the money we give to the poor, or in our prayers or our fasting, or in any other mark of faith. Our faith must be more real on the inside than it seems on the outside – not the other way round.

In the previous part of the Sermon on the Mount, Jesus has already argued for a complete change in how his listeners deal with a range of issues: anger and lust, retaliation, and making promises. Our inner motives are as important as our actions.

There is a profound revolution here. Religion is not to be about outward acts or appearances, but begins and ends with the transformation of the heart.

. . . .

PRAY

Eternal light, shine into our hearts,
eternal goodness, deliver us from evil,
eternal power, be our support,
eternal wisdom, scatter the darkness
of our ignorance,
eternal pity, have mercy upon us...
Alcuin of York (804)

. . . .

ACT

Review your disciplines of secret giving, secret prayer and secret fasting.

DAY 28
TESTING

READ Luke 4.1–13

'Jesus, full of the Holy Spirit, returned from the Jordan and was led by the Spirit in the wilderness, where for forty days he was tempted by the devil.'

....

REFLECT

Jesus' heart, too, was tested and tried at the beginning of his ministry. He spends 40 days in the wilderness after his baptism – partly seeking strength and partly being tested by the devil.

Three times, the devil comes to Jesus. The first

temptation is to use his power to serve himself. The second is to exchange earthly glory for truth. The third is to put God's purposes to the test. Jesus' final testing, which will come into focus several times during his ministry, is to turn aside from the way of the cross (Matthew 16.23; Luke 22.42).

The fact that Jesus endures this testing of the heart should encourage us. The Letter to the Hebrews says this: 'For we do not have a high priest who is unable to sympathize with our weaknesses, but we have one who in every respect has been tested as we are, yet without sin' (Hebrews 4.15).

. . . .

PRAY

Use this line of the Lord's Prayer today with the Bible passage in your mind:

'Lead us not into temptation but deliver us from evil.'

. . . .

ACT

Spend time praying for those you will meet today. How might you offer encouragement and strength to those who are being tested?

THE INNER LIFE

READ Mark 7.14–23

'there is nothing outside a person that by going in can defile, but the things that come out are what defile.'

. . . .

REFLECT

Again, Jesus changes our understanding of what it means to be fully human and live a good life. The religious people of his day were preoccupied with remaining pure. For them, that meant a strict dietary code and keeping away from certain kinds of people and practices. Remaining externally pure became more important than mercy.

Jesus abolishes all of this. He declares all foods clean. He eats with 'sinners' and undesirables of every kind. He heals on the Sabbath. Mercy triumphs over human custom and ritual; inner integrity is more important than reputation; and freedom of conscience is more precious than conforming to rules and tradition.

Jesus is not naïve about the capacity for evil in the human heart, which spoils and ruins lives. He is very clear that deep inner cleansing and renewal are needed, which go further and deeper than keeping to external rules. The only way to forgiveness, freedom and a pure heart is the way of the cross.

. . . .

PRAY

Lord Jesus Christ, you are the way,
the truth and the life:
let us not stray from you who are the way,
nor distrust your promises
who are the truth,
nor rest in anything but you
who are the life…
from a prayer of Erasmus (1536)

. . . .

ACT

Examine the rules you live by. Do any of them distract you from mercy or take away your freedom in Christ?

THE WAY OF HOLINESS

READ Galatians 5.16–26

'By contrast, the fruit of the Spirit is love, joy, peace, patience, kindness, generosity, faithfulness, gentleness, and self-control.'

. . . .

REFLECT

On good days, we long for our hearts to be made clean and pure. But we cannot make them so. Pure hearts flow from God's grace alone in Christ. We come to seek forgiveness and a new beginning through the cross.

Baptism is the sign of this once-and-for-all new beginning. Outwardly, we are washed in water as a sign of our inward spiritual cleansing through the cross. Outwardly, our old life dies and a new life begins.

That new life is a journey of change by the grace of God. The Spirit gradually works within us to bring out different qualities – Paul calls them fruits here. Like the Beatitudes, fruits are the character of Christ, formed within his people.

Slowly, God works within us by the Holy Spirit to form Christ in us and to help us become the people we are called to be.

. . . .

PRAY

Open our hearts
to the riches of your grace,
that we may bring forth
the fruit of the Spirit
in love and joy and peace;
through Jesus Christ your Son our Lord.
Collect for the Ninth Sunday after Trinity

. . . .

ACT

Talk to a Christian friend who is walking this journey with you. Ask one another what God is doing deep within through this reading of the Beatitudes.

'BLESSED ARE THE PEACEMAKERS, FOR THEY SHALL BE CALLED CHILDREN OF GOD'

DAY 31
PEACEMAKING

READ Matthew 5.1–10

'Blessed are the peacemakers, for they shall be called children of God.'

. . . .

REFLECT

Peace is a rich seam in Scripture. The Hebrew word for 'peace' is 'shalom'. It means much more than the absence of conflict. Shalom is flourishing wellbeing in relationships, in the nation and in creation.

Jesus comes to make peace. He heals those who are oppressed; forgives sins; and calms the storm.

Christ himself is our peace, creating one new humanity (Ephesians 2.14) and reconciling all things in himself through his death on the cross (Colossians 1.20). He is, indeed, the Prince of Peace (Isaiah 9.6).

But there is paradox here. Not everything can be reconciled. Christ brings judgement and division, as well as the promise of shalom.

The kind of peace Jesus makes is not the peace of a quiet life and of telling everyone exactly what they want to hear. The peace Jesus makes is the setting right of deep diseases – rewriting the code at the heart of the universe so that all may flourish.

. . . .

PRAY

Still your mind. Take time to listen to the words of Jesus and repeat them several times with the rhythm of your breathing:

'Blessed are the peacemakers,
for they shall be called children of God.'

. . . .

ACT

Are you able to identify a recent example of when you were a peacemaker? What did you learn from the experience?

LIVING WATER

READ John 4.1–30

'The water that I will give them will become in them a spring of water gushing up to eternal life.'

. . . .

REFLECT

The woman at the well in Samaria is without peace in her relationship with God her creator; in her chaotic personal life; and in her relationship with her local community (as she comes in the middle of the day to draw water when no one will be at the well). She is thirsty for something more in life. She represents many in our contemporary world.

Jesus reaches out to the woman and crosses barriers of gender, race, custom and religion in asking her for water, and then engaging her in lively conversation and serious debate. The Son of God is a peacemaker.

At the end of the story, the woman is reconciled to God, and understands the way of reconciliation

and forgiveness in her personal life and with her neighbours. Peace spreads like a spring rising and transforms the desert.

PRAY

O Divine Master,
grant that I may not so much seek
to be consoled as to console,
to be understood as to understand,
to be loved as to love.
A Franciscan Prayer

ACT

Think of three people in your own networks who seem not to be at peace. Pray for them and imagine ways in which you can connect with them.

THE FATHER'S LOVE

READ Luke 15.11–32

'But while he was still far off, his father saw him and was filled with compassion; he ran and put his arms around him and kissed him.'

. . . .

REFLECT

One of Jesus' best-known parables describes the God who loves to make peace. The father in the story is generous to both his sons.

The younger brother takes his inheritance, travels to a far country and wastes it. He falls into poverty and makes the long journey home. His father is watching for him to return and runs to welcome him back not as a slave, but as a son. Peace is made.

The older brother has forgotten his father's love, despite remaining in the family home. He resents the return of his younger brother. His father comes out and pleads with him. He invites him back into the feast. We do not know how the story ends.

God is seeking the return of his children to a full and mature relationship of love; both those who have rebelled outwardly and those who have rebelled inwardly. We are called to live together in unity and love.

. . . .

PRAY

Behold how good and pleasant it is
to dwell together in unity...
For there the Lord
has promised his blessing:
even life for evermore.
Psalm 133

. . . .

ACT

Can you identify 'older brothers' and 'younger brothers' in the life of your own community? How can you work for reconciliation?

DAY 34
RESTORATION

READ John 21.15–19

'Simon son of John, do you love me more than these?'

. . . .

REFLECT

Every Christian experiences moments of failure when we fall short. In those times, God is patient with us. We do not lose God's love or God's friendship.

Simon Peter has denied even knowing Jesus three times at the point of his greatest need (John 18.25–27). But the risen Jesus reaches out to him after the breakfast on the beach. Jesus takes

Peter back to the beginning. He is no longer 'the rock', but simply 'Simon son of John'. Three times, Jesus invites Simon to declare his love. Simon does so but with humility, not extravagant boasting. Three times, Jesus commissions Peter to tend and feed his flock.

After the commission comes the simple invitation to renew his call: 'Follow me.' Not literally this time. Imitate me. Do what I do. Lead the Church this way.

The Christian life is not an even journey. In the moments when we fall, we need each other.

. . . .

PRAY

Almighty Father, who in your great mercy gladdened the disciples with the sight of the risen Lord: give us such knowledge of his presence with us, that we may be strengthened and sustained by his risen life...
Collect for the Third Sunday of Easter

. . . .

ACT

Who are the people to whom you turn when you fall and find the way difficult?

THE RECONCILIATION OF ALL THINGS

READ Colossians 1.15–23

*'and through him God was pleased
to reconcile to himself all things,
whether on earth or in heaven,
by making peace through the blood
of his cross.'*

. . . .

REFLECT

This part of Colossians is probably an early hymn or creed used in worship. It has a very rich and deep understanding of Christ. Everything in creation is made through Christ and is sustained by Christ. God's fullness dwells in Christ.

More than that, everything in all creation is reconciled in Christ through his death on the cross. The cross is the means of the healing not just of individuals, nor simply of communities or even nations. The cross is a profound mystery and the central point of history: God's means of reconciling the whole of creation.

Making peace is at the very heart of God's mission. This is the reason Jesus Christ came. We read the seventh beatitude with new understanding. This is why we, too, are called to be peacemakers and children of God.

. . . .

PRAY

Almighty God,
from whom all thoughts
of truth and peace proceed:
kindle, we pray, in the hearts of all,
the true love of peace...
Collect for the Peace of the World

. . . .

ACT

How will this seventh beatitude shape the journey of your life today and in the years to come?

DAYS 36 TO 40

'BLESSED ARE THOSE WHO SUFFER PERSECUTION FOR RIGHTEOUSNESS' SAKE, FOR THEIRS IS THE KINGDOM OF HEAVEN'

FINDING COURAGE

READ Matthew 5.1–12

'Blessed are those who suffer persecution for righteousness' sake, for theirs is the kingdom of heaven.'

. . . .

REFLECT

Who is Jesus? Jesus is poor in spirit, mourning, hungry for justice, humble, ready to forgive, full of integrity and a peacemaker. There is one other key quality in his life: the readiness to suffer for what is right is the cornerstone of his ministry. Jesus is willing to bear the cost of proclaiming the good news. Jesus is willing to die for the sins of the whole world to bring mercy and peace, wholeness and justice.

This is the only beatitude to be expanded in two verses of commentary which fill out its meaning (verses 11 and 12 – sometimes read as a ninth beatitude).

The gospels unfold for us the ways in which Jesus faced opposition and insult from the very beginning

of his ministry, especially in the story of his passion
which Christians remember each year in Holy Week.
It is this willingness to suffer that reshapes the world.

. . . .

PRAY

Still your mind. Take time to listen to the
words of Jesus and repeat them several
times with the rhythm of your breathing:

*'Blessed are those who suffer persecution
for righteousness' sake,
for theirs is the kingdom of heaven.'*

. . . .

ACT

Reflect today on this last beatitude and on
the commentary in verses 11 and 12 as you
contemplate the passion of Jesus.

THE JOURNEY TO THE CROSS

READ Matthew 16.13–28

'Jesus began to show his disciples that he must go to Jerusalem and undergo great suffering…'

. . . .

REFLECT

This key passage in Matthew is a commentary on the eighth beatitude. The disciples recognize that Jesus is the Messiah, the Son of God. They have lived with him and watched him and seen his beautiful character.

The disciples are expecting a Messiah who will begin to reign as king in Jerusalem. But Jesus has a deeper, wider vision: the Son of God must suffer and die and be raised to life. God is seeking to mend and heal the whole of creation in every generation, not simply establish a human kingdom in one time and place.

In each of the gospels, the disciples struggle to accept and believe this deeper vision. But Jesus then calls them even further. They, too, must share this mission. The disciples of Jesus are also called to walk in the way of the cross and to lose their lives for the sake of the gospel.

. . . .

PRAY

Mercifully grant that we,
walking in the way of the cross,
may find it none other
than the way of life and peace;
through Jesus Christ your Son our Lord.
Collect for the Third Sunday of Lent

. . . .

ACT

Look around your networks for those whose Christian life is costly at the moment. Say or do something today to encourage someone.

AT THE FOOT OF THE CROSS

READ John 19.16–30

'When Jesus had received the wine, he said, "It is finished." Then he bowed his head and gave up his spirit.'

. . . .

REFLECT

Here is the central question of the gospels. Jesus was the most complete human person ever to have lived. His life brought immense blessing. Why was it cut short by such a cruel and terrible death? And why does Jesus regard his own death as his main task? His final words from the cross are 'It is finished', now that it has been accomplished.

The answer lies in the immense and powerful meaning in his death for the sins of the world. Here is full and complete forgiveness and healing for the sins of the entire world and the deep flaws in the heart of creation. Here is the way God brings together this fractured and divided world and opens up the way to eternal life.

A fundamental part of being human is being willing
to bear the cost of what you believe: not to bend to
the dictates of fashion, or to please others,
or to avoid suffering. Only in this way can we fulfil
our destiny and make a lasting contribution
to the world. Take courage.

PRAY

Look with mercy on this your family
for which our Lord Jesus Christ
was content to be betrayed
and given up into the hands of sinners
and to suffer death upon the cross...
Collect for Good Friday

ACT

What are the challenges you will need
to face in your Christian life as you
look ahead? Write down your sources of
strength and courage for facing them.

WALKING WITH THE RISEN CHRIST

READ Luke 24.13–35

'Was it not necessary that the Messiah should suffer these things then and enter into his glory?'

. . . .

REFLECT

Jesus draws near to two disciples on the first Easter morning as they walk away from Jerusalem in their grief. Slowly, they recognize him through the gift of friendship and community, as they explore the scriptures together and in the breaking of the bread.

In this passage, the poor in spirit are blessed. The mourning are comforted. The peacemaker restores these two disciples to the community in Jerusalem.

Those whose hearts are pure see God. The fearful find hope and courage.

The Beatitudes only make sense because the death of Jesus is not the end of the story. Suffering and death give way to resurrection and joy. Jesus' own resurrection is the most powerful sign of all that death will be reversed for all who trust in Christ. The promises of the Beatitudes rest on resurrection. Death and decay and despair are overcome.
A new song of hope begins.

· ·

PRAY

Almighty Father,
who in your great mercy gladdened the
disciples with the sight of the risen Lord:
give us such knowledge of his presence
with us, that we may be strengthened
and sustained by his risen life...
Collect for the Third Sunday of Easter

· ·

ACT

Sing psalms and hymns and spiritual songs today (and every day if you can) as a celebration of resurrection.

BAPTIZED INTO HIS DEATH

READ Romans 6.1–14

'Therefore we have been buried with him by baptism into death... so we too might walk in newness of life.'

. . . .

REFLECT

Jesus gives the Beatitudes to his disciples as the very first part of his teaching in the Sermon on the Mount. The eight qualities of the Beatitudes describe the character of Christ and the abundant, authentic life to which everyone is called. They set out a vision for the Church of Jesus Christ in every generation.

All down the centuries, Christians have listened to the

Beatitudes across the 40 days of Lent as part of our preparation for baptism and as part of our renewal of baptismal promises at Easter or in confirmation.

In baptism, we are buried with Christ to be raised with him. We are called to walk in newness of life and in resurrection; to be poor in spirit; compassionate; servants to all; seeking justice; merciful; living from the inside out; making peace; and willing to bear the cost of our discipleship. This is what it means to be a Christian. How will this shape the journey of your life?

PRAY

By the power of your Holy Spirit you give your faithful people new life in the water of baptism. Guide and strengthen us by the same Spirit, that we who are born again may serve you in faith and love, and grow into the full stature of your Son, Jesus Christ...
The Collect for Baptism

ACT

Look back over these 40 days of readings. What have you learned? What will you take with you?

NEXT STEPS

CONTINUE THE JOURNEY WITH THE LORD'S PRAYER

Those using this material for LentPilgrim 2019 are invited to continue with the **EasterPilgrim** journey from Easter Day to Ascension. The reflections for these 40 Days – found in *Pilgrim Journeys: The Lord's Prayer* from Church House Publishing – can be used at any time, but make an ideal preparation for **Thy Kingdom Come**, the global prayer movement, from Ascension to Pentecost.

For further details, visit **www.churchofengland.org/Easter**

JOIN A LOCAL GROUP USING THE 'PILGRIM' COURSE

Pilgrim: A Course for the Christian Journey is widely used across and beyond the Church of England. *Pilgrim* offers eight short courses designed to be used by small groups of people who are exploring the Christian faith. The course is based around four core texts, including The Beatitudes. Find out more about *Pilgrim* books, eBooks, DVDs and online resources at **www.pilgrimcourse.org**

A COURSE FOR THE CHRISTIAN JOURNEY

JOIN IN WITH FURTHER DISCIPLESHIP CAMPAIGNS

Visit **www.churchofengland.org/Lent** to sign up (by e-mail or text) to take part in future discipleship initiatives for Easter 2019 and beyond from the Church of England. It is free to sign up and you can easily opt out at any time.

THE CHURCH OF ENGLAND